This book is dedicated to my children - Mikey, Kobe, and Jojo.

Copyright © 2024 Grow Grit Press LLC. All rights reserved. No part of this book may be reproduced in any form without permission in writing from the publisher. Please send bulk order requests to info@ninjalifehacks.tv

Paperback ISBN: 978-1-63731-913-0
Hardcover ISBN: 978-1-63731-915-4
eBook ISBN: 978-1-63731-914-7

Printed and bound in the USA.
NinjaLifeHacks.tv

Ninja Life Hacks®
by Mary Nhin

Kind Ninja
and the Buddy Bench

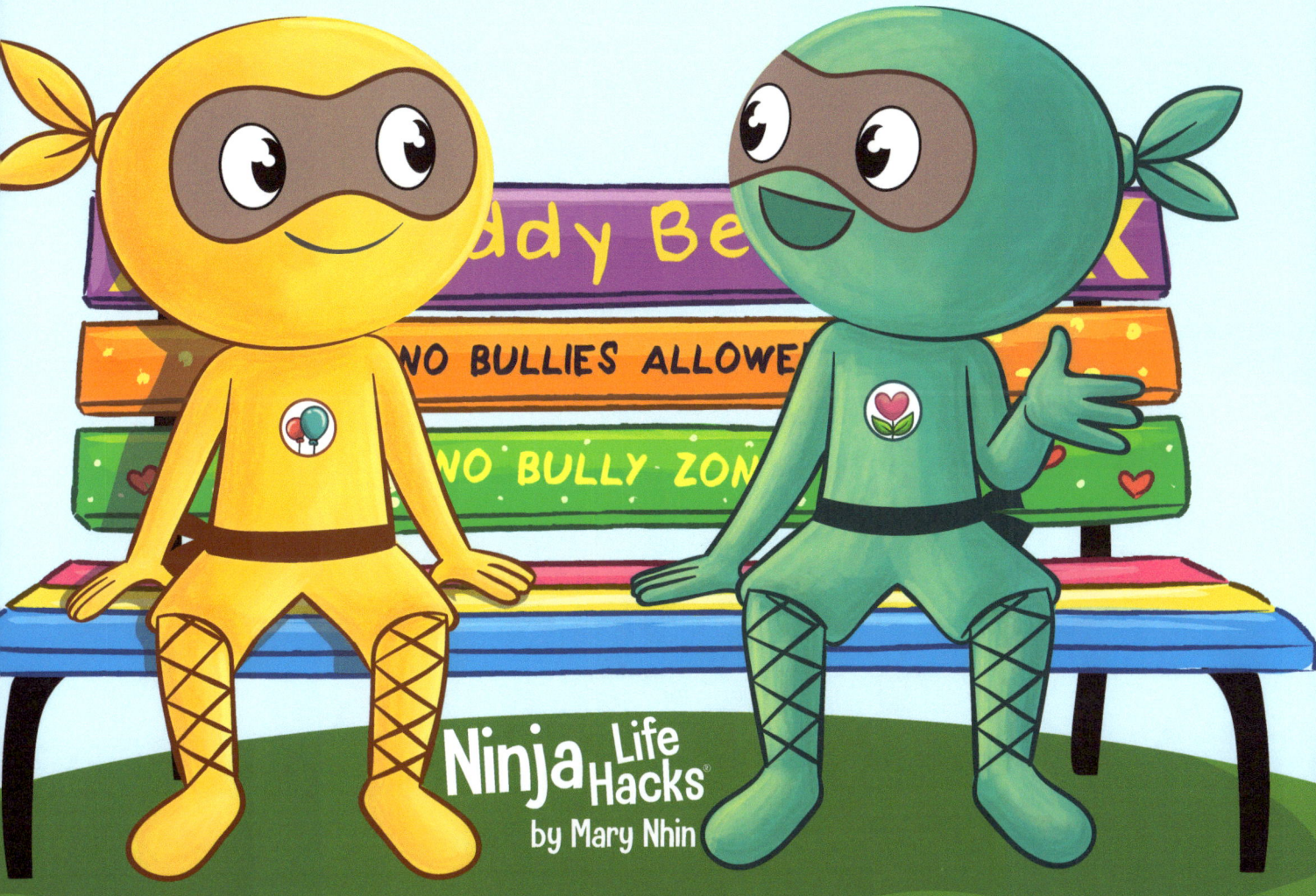

Ninja Life Hacks®
by Mary Nhin

We gathered some wood, nails, and paint,
I was so excited, I could hardly wait!
With hammers and brushes, we started to build,
A bench of bright colors, we were so thrilled.

I pounded the nails with a clumsy whack,
Got paint on my clothes, even my back!
But it was fun, and we laughed a lot,
The buddy bench was exactly what we sought.

"Come join us," I said, with a friendly grin,
She smiled back and then joined in.
We kicked a ball and climbed a tree,
The buddy bench helped her feel free.

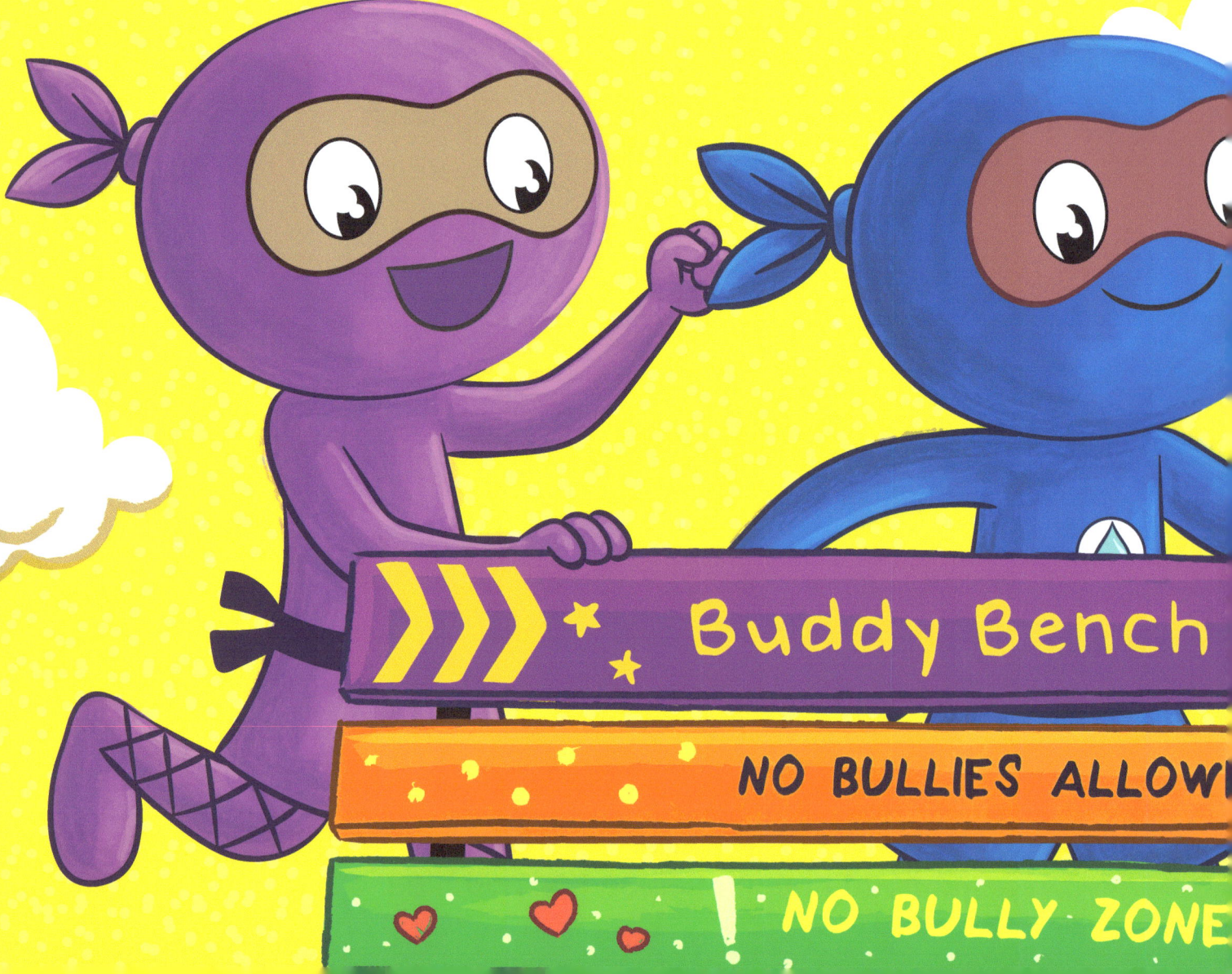

So if you see someone who's feeling alone,
Remember Kind Ninja and the buddy bench shown.
A little kindness goes a long way,
Bringing smiles and friends every day.

www.ingramcontent.com/pod-product-compliance
Lightning Source LLC
Chambersburg PA
CBHW041714160426
43209CB00018B/1828